Pebble® Plus

MILITARY BRANCHES
THE U.S. COAST GUARD

by Matt Doeden

Consulting Editor: Gail Saunders-Smith, PhD

Consultant: Lt. Tony Migliorini
U.S. Coast Guard, Community Relations

Capstone press®

Mankato, Minnesota

Pebble Plus is published by Capstone Press,
151 Good Counsel Drive, P.O. Box 669, Mankato, Minnesota 56002.
www.capstonepress.com

1 2 3 4 5 6 13 12 11 10 09 08

Library of Congress Cataloging-in-Publication Data
Doeden, Matt.
    The U.S. Coast Guard / by Matt Doeden.
    p. cm. — (Pebble Plus. Military branches)
    Includes bibliographical references and index.
    ISBN-13: 978-1-4296-1734-5 (hardcover)
    ISBN-10: 1-4296-1734-9 (hardcover)
    1. United States. Coast Guard — Juvenile literature. I. Title. II. Series.
VG53.D64 2009
363.28'60973 — dc22   2008001753

Summary: Simple text and photographs describe the U.S. Coast Guard's purpose, jobs, and machines.

Editorial Credits
Gillia Olson, editor; Renée T. Doyle, designer; Jo Miller, photo researcher

Photo Credits
AP Images/David J. Phillip, 19; U.S. Marine Corps/Lcpl David J. Blake, 13
Corbis/Reuters/Chip East, 7
iStockphoto/Lari Kemilainen, 3
Photo by Ted Carlson/Fotodynamics, 11, 21
Photo courtesy of Northrop Grumman, 17
Shutterstock/Patsy A. Jacks, 1
U.S. Coast Guard photo by George Gotschalk, 9; by Linda Vetter, front and back cover, 22; by PA3 Adam Eggers,
    15; by Petty Officer Jonathan R. Cilley, 5

Artistic Effects
iStockphoto/Brandon Seidel (water), cover, 1, 24
iStockphoto/Plainview (metal), cover, 1

Note to Parents and Teachers

The Military Branches set supports national science standards related to science,
technology, and society. This book describes and illustrates the U.S. Coast Guard. The
images support early readers in understanding the text. The repetition of words and
phrases helps early readers learn new words. This book also introduces early readers to
subject-specific vocabulary words, which are defined in the Glossary section. Early
readers may need assistance to read some words and to use the Table of Contents,
Glossary, Read More, Internet Sites, and Index sections of the book.

Table of Contents

What Is the Coast Guard?

The Coast Guard

is a branch of the

United States Armed Forces.

The Coast Guard protects

the country's shores.

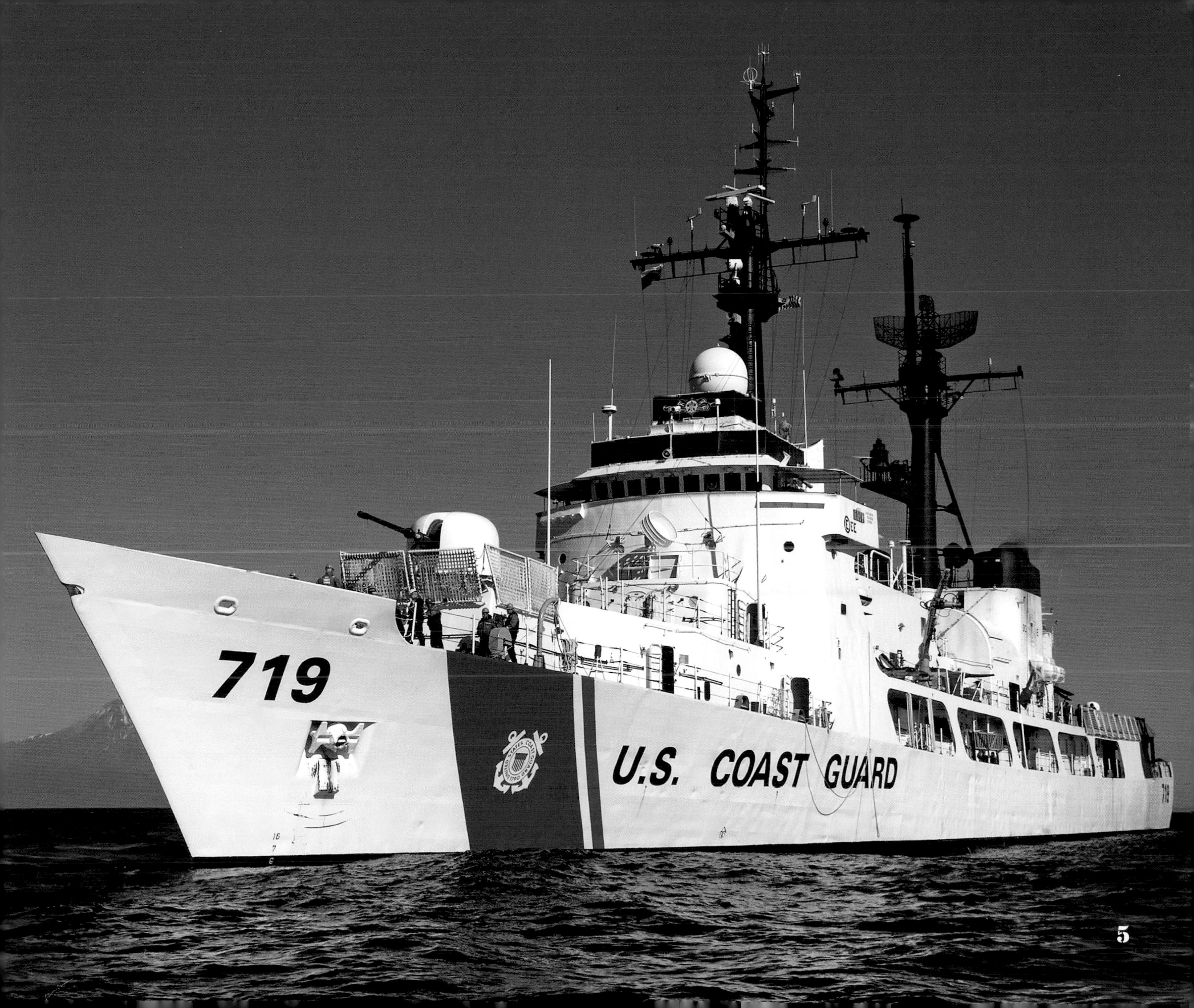

719
U.S. COAST GUARD

Coast Guard Jobs

Coast Guard ships

have crews.

The captain or another officer

gives orders to the crew.

Coast Guard police uphold

the law at sea.

They use Defender Class

boats to catch lawbreakers.

Coast Guard pilots fly
helicopters or airplanes.
They use Dolphin helicopters
to stop lawbreakers.

In emergencies, Coast Guard
medics help people
who are hurt.

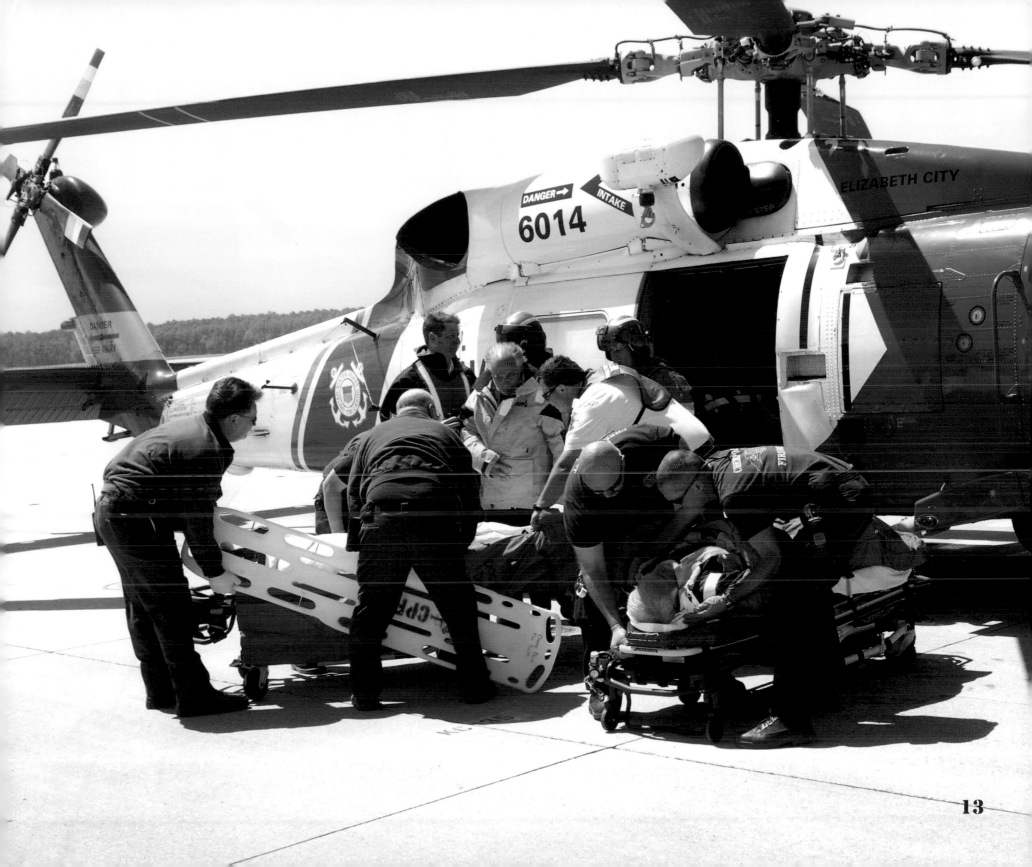

Coast Guard Machines

Large Coast Guard ships

are called cutters.

Cutters go far out to sea.

Smaller boats stay

near shore.

Coast Guard airplanes

search large areas

of water or land.

The C-130J is

a Coast Guard airplane.

Coast Guard helicopters

rescue people.

The Jayhawk is

a rescue helicopter.

Keeping Us Safe

The brave men and women

of the Coast Guard

watch our shores.

Their teamwork keeps us safe.

Glossary

Armed Forces — the whole military; the U.S. Armed Forces include the Army, Navy, Air Force, Marine Corps, and Coast Guard.

branch — a part of a larger group

captain — the leader on a ship

crew — a team of people who work together

medic — someone trained to give medical help in an emergency

officer — someone who is in charge of other people

protect — to keep safe

rescue — to save someone who is in danger

shore — land that touches a lake, ocean, or other body of water

Read More

Braulick, Carrie A. *The U.S. Coast Guard.* The U.S. Armed Forces. Mankato, Minn.: Capstone Press, 2005.

Braulick, Carrie A. *U.S. Coast Guard Cutters.* Military Vehicles. Mankato, Minn.: Capstone Press, 2007.

Randolph, Joanne. *Coast Guard Boats.* To The Rescue! New York: PowerKids Press, 2008.

Internet Sites

FactHound offers a safe, fun way to find Internet sites related to this book. All of the sites on FactHound have been researched by our staff.

Here's how:

1. Visit *www.facthound.com*

2. Choose your grade level.

3. Type in this book ID **1429617349** for age-appropriate sites. You may also browse subjects by clicking on letters, or by clicking on pictures and words.

4. Click on the **Fetch It** button.

FactHound will fetch the best sites for you!

Index

Word Count: 137
Grade: 1
Early-Intervention Level: 23